30 Days of
Choosing
Gratitude

*Every time I hear the word grace,
I am reminded that I must live a life, every day,
which reflects my gratitude to God.*

Charles W. Colson[1]

Nancy DeMoss Wolgemuth

'm so glad you've decided to join me on this journey toward a heart of gratitude! I've been seeking to cultivate this characteristic in my own life, and I want you to see what I've seen. I want you to experience the fresh joys I am encountering on a daily basis!

I truly believe a grateful spirit, rooted in the soil of God's goodness and grace, will radically impact how you view and respond to everything in your life. As we explore this simple but profound trait called gratitude over the next thirty days, I pray it will be for you a journey to greater freedom and joy—a journey closer to the heart of God.

By going through each day's reading, I'm encouraging you to concentrate on cultivating the attitude of gratitude for thirty days. You'll need about twenty to thirty minutes each day, preferably at a time and in a place with minimal distractions. To get the most out of your time, here are two things you'll want to do:

1. Use your Bible. Each day includes a passage to look up. Don't just skim through it. Savor it. Meditate on it. Ask the Holy Spirit to highlight words and phrases that can be invested in your memory bank. It will be *His* words—not mine—that will transform you into a grateful person.

2. Write down what God's doing in your life. Use this journal to keep track of your journey. Here are some suggestions for how to do that:

> *Gratitude in Action*—Record your responses to the questions and assignments.

> *Key Thought*—Record a key thought and any further insight you gain from each day's Scripture reading.

> *Gratitude List*—Each day, make a list of five things you're thankful for. As you look for new things to include, you'll be amazed at how your eyes are opened to see His mercies that are "new every morning" (Lam. 3:22–23).

> *Insights*—Capture any additional insights and Scriptures the Lord shows you about gratitude as you make this a focus of your thinking. Record how you're doing as you seek to cultivate a grateful heart. Identify what the Lord shows you along the way—heart issues that need to be addressed, "triggers" to ingratitude that you need to watch out for, helps in becoming more grateful, consequences of ingratitude and blessings of gratitude, the impact of grateful people on those around them, etc.

This thirty-day guide includes a lot of practical exercises designed to help you become a more thankful person. But don't get so preoccupied with trying to answer every question, complete every "assignment," and make every list that you miss the heart of the matter. These are just suggestions. If you find a particular question or project isn't helpful . . . move on to the next one! The point is to let the Lord speak to you through His Word, and to respond to Him in humility and obedience, as you seek to make gratitude a way of life.

Okay, let's get started!

Nancy

Nancy DeMoss Wolgemuth

[1] Ellen Vaughn, *Radical Gratitude* (Grand Rapids: Zondervan, 2005), 10 (from the foreword by Charles W. Colson).

Scripture Reading: Colossians 3:12–17

I've often said that gratitude is learning to recognize and express appreciation for the benefits we have received from God and from others. Let's break down these components a bit further:

To "recognize" what we receive each day, the eyes of our heart must be open and alert. This means constantly being on the lookout for blessings, making each day a treasure hunt. I have a friend who makes a habit of thanking the Lord for ten things every morning before he gets out of bed. He wants to start his day by focusing on the goodness of God, rather than whatever problems or challenges he may have to deal with that day.

To "express appreciation" means that what's in our heart needs to come out! It means being intentional about thanking God and others for the blessings that come our way. It also means frequent opportunities to invest back into those who are involved in our lives. It's our return gift to them—and to the Lord.

Being mindful of "the benefits we have received" helps squeeze bitterness and entitlement from our hearts, replacing negative, depressing thoughts with the realization that our loving Father has showered us with good things and that even the "bad things" in our lives are "benefits," intended to make us more like Jesus.

Gratitude changes the way we start the day, spend the day, and look back on the day. It defines us as people who value our relationship with God and with those He's placed around us. By thanking Him and others throughout the day, we are expressing humility, realizing these "benefits" are all undeserved.

Gratitude in Action:

1. Overall, how would you rate your "Gratitude Quotient"? (If you're not sure—or you want to know how others would answer that question about you—ask a couple people who live or work with you . . . people you know

will be honest with you!) Check any of the following that apply:

☐ I look at the world through grateful eyes and consistently express my gratitude to God and others.

☐ I know I've been greatly blessed, but I don't often stop to actually express my gratitude to God and others.

☐ To be honest, I had not thought a lot about gratitude until starting this devotional. I've got a long way to go to develop a lifestyle of gratitude.

☐ I'm a whiner! I tend to focus on my problems, and I frequently express them to others.

2. Write a prayer asking the Lord to cultivate in you a more grateful heart over these next thirty days. If you have realized that your "Gratitude Quotient" is not what it should be, confess your ungrateful spirit to the Lord. Ask Him to forgive you and to transform you by the power of His Spirit into a truly thankful person.

3. Write down and memorize the definition of gratitude at the beginning of today's reading, and review it whenever you're feeling less than thankful about where you are and what's going on.

Key Thought:

_____

_____

Gratitude List:

_____

_____

Insights:

_____

_____

Scripture Reading: *Colossians 1:3, 12; 2:7; 3:15–17; 4:2*

Every chapter in Paul's letter to the Colossians has at least one reference to the attitude of gratitude. In your Bible, underline or circle the words "thank," "thanks," "thanksgiving," "thankful," and "thankfulness" in the verses above.

Paul makes it clear that being thankful is not optional. We learn about the source, the nature, the frequency, the object, and the scope of thankfulness, and we are introduced to its companions. Record in your journal as many insights about Christian gratitude as you can find, from the above verses in Colossians.

The central theme of Colossians is *Christ.* He is exalted and worshiped for

- His divine nature
- being the Creator and Sustainer of all things
- His preeminence over all creation and over all cosmic rulers and powers
- His redemptive, reconciling work on the cross
- defeating the powers of darkness
- being the Head of the Church which is His Body
- being the fulfillment and substance of Old Testament types and figures
- being the believer's life and our hope of glory
- and so much more!

As those who have "died" with Christ, "been buried with him in baptism," and "raised with him through faith," our joy and hope do not emanate from any earthly source or from our religious practices, but from *Him.*

Within the four chapters of this short epistle, Paul calls us to be: sexually pure, compassionate, kind, humble, meek, patient, forgiving, loving, peaceful, obedient, just, wise, gracious, and *thankful! Whew*—that's a tall order! But everything we are called to be and do as "Christians" flows out of who *Christ* is in us, and what He has already done on our behalf.

As Christ abounds in His infinite splendor and in His grace toward us, so when we walk by faith in Him, we have abundant motivation—and divine enabling—to live a life that is always "abounding in thanksgiving."

Gratitude in Action:

As is the case regarding every virtue and everything that is expected of us as children of God, true thankfulness is rooted and grounded in Christ and His gospel. It is generated by His life within us. Read through one or more of the following passages from Colossians, meditating on them, praying them back to God, and using them as a basis for giving thanks to Him (I've helped you get started on the first one):

- 1:12–14—*Oh Father, I am so grateful and joyfully give you thanks, because though I was in no way related to you and had no right to have any part in your kingdom, by your grace, you have made me fit (qualified) to be a recipient, along with others who belong to your family, of the infinite riches of your inheritance.*

- 1:15–22

- 2:9–15

- 3:1–11

Key Thought:

_____

_____

Gratitude List:

_____

_____

Insights:

_____

Scripture Reading: Psalm 107:1–32

The theme of Psalm 107 is stated in the first two verses:

> ¹*Oh give thanks to the* LORD, *for he is good,*
> *for his steadfast love endures forever!*
> ²*Let the redeemed of the* LORD *say so,*
> *whom he has redeemed from trouble . . .*

This theme is followed by four "personal testimonies"—illustrations of those who have been redeemed by the Lord and have reason to give Him thanks. Each testimony includes a similar progression:

- Distress—the straits people found themselves in
- Desperate cry to the Lord for help
- Divine deliverance

The passage is punctuated by a response—a "thanksgiving chorus" that is repeated at the end of each testimony (vv. 8, 15, 21, 31). Write out the words to that chorus in your journal.

How often do you consciously thank the Lord for His steadfast mercy and love and His "wondrous works" in your life?

Gratitude in Action:

1. Write out your personal testimony of God's saving grace, following the progression found in Psalm 107.

   - What was your life like before He redeemed you? (If you need help getting started, take a look at Ephesians 2:1–3.)

   - How did God bring you to the end of yourself, to the place where you cried out to Him for mercy?

- What has changed in your life since He delivered you from your slavery to sin?

2. If you have additional time, write another brief testimony of a time subsequent to your initial salvation, when you were in distress, you cried out to the Lord, and He came to your rescue.

3. Now, re-read the first two verses of Psalm 107 and the "chorus" that recurs throughout. Take time to thank the Lord for His steadfast love and His redeeming work in your life.

4. *"Let the redeemed of the LORD say so . . ."* (v. 2). Share your story *(His* story) with someone else today. Tell them how grateful you are to the Lord for saving you—eternally, as well as daily.

Key Thought:

_____

_____

_____

Gratitude List:

_____

_____

_____

Insights:

_____

_____

_____

Scripture Reading: *Psalm 103:1–5*

I recently interviewed a woman for our *Revive Our Hearts* broadcast who has faithfully memorized and meditated on Scripture for more than fifty years. She talked about the many benefits she has received as a result of hiding God's Word in her heart.

I was amazed when she mentioned that she had never really been depressed. She explained that whenever she finds herself becoming a bit down or blue, she begins to quote Psalm 103. At which point in the interview, she proceeded to recite the entire psalm—from memory, thoughtfully, with heartfelt expression.

It was a moving experience for all of us who were in the room listening. When she got to the end of the passage, there was a holy hush. The first thought that went through my mind was, *How in the world could anyone ever be overwhelmed with depression, and how in the world could I ever give in to discouragement, if all these blessings are ours—and they are!*

As we recognize and identify the specific blessings we have received from God and from others, we discover countless reasons for expressing gratitude. The Psalmist took time to bless the Lord for specific benefits—he didn't want to forget even one of them! As you open your heart to Him in prayer today, ask God to reveal to you just how great your "benefits package" really is.

Designate several pages in your journal or notebook for each of these two headings: "Gifts from God" and "Gifts from Others." Then start making a list of everything that comes to mind. As you try filling these in with personal examples, it's quite natural for your writing to stop and start, sometimes piling up faster than you can get the blessings down, sometimes drawing a blank about what to put next. So don't try forcing this into a one-time, ten-minute exercise. Keep adding to these lists as additional gifts come to mind over the next thirty days (and beyond!).

Gratitude in Action:

1. After you've written out a list of your blessings, take some time to walk through your list line by line, thanking God for each of these "benefits."

2. Read Psalm 103 aloud. Try memorizing and meditating on at least the first five verses over the next week or so.

Key Thought:

_____

_____

_____

_____

Gratitude List:

_____

_____

_____

_____

Insights:

_____

_____

_____

_____

Scripture Reading: *Ephesians 5:15–21*

Since starting to catalogue some of your blessings yesterday, I hope you're becoming more alert to the many reasons you have to be grateful. But I'm reminded of that visual illustration about the jar filled with rocks. The speaker asks, "Would you say this jar is full?" Yes. "Is there any way it could hold any more?" No. But by continuing to add smaller pieces of rock and sand, we soon discover there was more room inside than we realized.

I remember hearing a friend tell how, while brushing his teeth one morning and meditating on one of the verses in today's reading (Eph. 5:20), he was struck by the word "everything." He was reminded of the importance of thanking God for even those "little things" that we often overlook. It made him pause and be thankful for, well . . . his toothbrush. And his toothpaste. And, while he was at it, he thanked God for his teeth, for probably the first time in his life.

This may require another separate list from the ones you made yesterday, but it's definitely a category worth considering. Since everything is a gift from God (James 1:17), "everything" is something to be thankful for.

My friend told me he also asked himself: "If tomorrow's supply depended on today's thanksgiving, how much would I have tomorrow?" Something to think about!

Gratitude in Action:

1. What "little things" can you add to the gratitude lists you've started?

2. Some of the items on your "everything" list will make you realize you've taken certain people in your life for granted. Say thank you today in some way.

Key Thought:

_____
_____
_____
_____
_____

Gratitude List:

_____
_____
_____
_____
_____

Insights:

_____
_____
_____
_____
_____

Day 6: *Top Ten*

Scripture Reading: *Romans 11:33–36*

Robertson McQuilkin, former president of Columbia International University, tells of a time when, following his wife's diagnosis with Alzheimer's and the death of his eldest son, he retreated alone to a mountain hideaway, trying to reorient his heart and recapture a love for God that had slowly evaporated in the heat of personal, tragic loss.

It certainly didn't happen in the first five minutes, but after a day devoted to prayer and fasting, he began writing God a love letter, enumerating the gifts he had received from the Lord's hand, worshiping Him with pen and paper. In this season of revival, he identified ten particular blessings from God that just absolutely exceeded his imagination, things he could hardly find words to express how invaluable they were, how impossible life would be without them.

I like that. In fact, I encourage you to flip back through the lists you've been making the last few days and choose a top ten or so—a highlight reel of spiritual blessings that are so big, you could never generate enough gratitude to express what they mean to you and what they tell you about your Savior.

See if, like Robertson McQuilkin, you find your heart for God renewed by what he called "the reflex action of thanksgiving. My love flamed up from the dying embers and my spirit soared. I discovered that ingratitude impoverishes—but that a heavy heart lifts on the wings of praise."[1]

Gratitude in Action:

Since a whole lifetime isn't enough to say thanks for these blessings, the next time your mind is troubled by sad or worrisome thoughts, pull out your top ten and consciously transfer your focus from whatever is weighing you down, and start giving thanks for the things on your list.

Key Thought:

_____

_____

_____

_____

_____

Gratitude List:

_____

_____

_____

_____

Insights:

_____

_____

_____

_____

_____

[1] R.J. Morgan, *Nelson's Complete Book of Stories, Illustrations, and Quotes,* electronic ed. (Nashville: Thomas Nelson, 2000), 814.

Scripture Reading: *Luke 17:11-15*

In the account of Jesus' healing of the ten lepers, I want you to notice a few things that distinguished the one who returned to say "thank you" to Jesus.

First, he came loudly. This was no private matter, nor was it a quiet one-on-one conversation with Jesus off in a corner somewhere. "One of them, when he saw that he was healed, turned back, *praising God with a loud voice*" (Luke 17:15). This man just couldn't contain his gratitude. This occasion called for an unrestrained, extreme, public display of thanks.

Oh, for such a grateful spirit as we see in this man. May the volume of our gratitude be cranked high not only when we're asking for help (as all ten of the lepers had done) but also when acknowledging our Helper. May our giving of thanks be as obvious and expressive as our sharing of needs!

I think of my Dad, whose frequent response I mentioned earlier—"I'm doing *better than I deserve.*" I think of my dear friend "Mom Johnson," now in heaven after living a long earthly life of ninety-two years, who would often say, "I have more blessings than problems." I think of the most buoyant, approachable people I know—the ones I love spending time with, who bless and enrich my life whenever I am around them. It's not that they have the fewest problems, or the cleanest histories, or the most obvious reasons for happiness. They're simply the ones who are "loudest" about giving thanks, who are not always reciting a long list of problems, complaints, and criticisms but who choose to be grateful. They know they've already been given more than life could ever cost them. The Lord keeps them full despite the world's best attempts at depleting them. And they don't mind telling you about it.

I want to be one of those people, don't you?

Second, he came close. We never get any closer to Jesus than when we come with humble gratitude. The ten lepers who first met Jesus "stood at a distance" (v. 12)—lepers were ceremonially defiled and were not allowed to come close to those who were "clean." The healed leper who "fell on his face at Jesus' feet, giving him thanks"

(v. 16) was the only one of the ten who ever got close to Jesus. Gratitude places us in close proximity to Christ, where we experience the fullness of His redeeming power and enjoy the blessing of His presence.

Third, he came from a distance. "He was a Samaritan" (v. 16). Unlike some of us who can't remember a time when we weren't at least somewhat aware of God's presence and power, this man had never known the true God until Jesus came into His world and transformed his life. After being separated from Jesus by a religious, cultural, and physical gulf, he loved what he saw in Jesus—up close and personal. Do you love what you see in Jesus? Gratitude will help bridge the distance and draw you close to Jesus.

Think today, not only about what you have to be grateful for, but about the blessings we receive when we take time to stop and express our gratitude to God and others.

Gratitude in Action:

Look for an opportunity today to thank the Lord for what He has done in your life—aloud, and in the presence of one or more others. And don't whisper your prayer—speak up! You may feel a bit awkward if you're not accustomed to praise Him in this way. But think about how you express yourself when you are enthused or earnest about something in another realm of your life—say, being surprised with an engagement ring, receiving a promotion at work, or your kid's soccer game.

Key Thought:

_____

Gratitude List:

_____

Insights:

_____

Scripture Reading: James 4:6–10

Members of the Masai tribe in West Africa understand that gratitude and humility go hand in hand. When they want to say "thank you," they touch their forehead down to the ground and say, literally, "My head is in the dirt."

Another African tribe expresses gratitude in a similar way by saying, "I sit on the ground before you." When someone wants to make his gratitude known, he goes and just sits quietly for a period of time in front of the hut of the person to whom he is grateful.

One of the fundamental qualities invariably found in a grateful person is *humility*. Gratitude is the overflow of a humble heart, just as surely as an ungrateful, complaining spirit flows out of a proud heart.

Proud people are wrapped up in themselves. They think much of themselves and little of others. If people or circumstances don't please or suit them, they are prone to "whine" or become resentful. Today's reading reminds us that "God opposes the proud"—the concept is that He stiff-arms them, He keeps them at a distance, He "sets Himself in battle array" against them.

But when we choose to "humble ourselves," as we are exhorted in James 4, God draws near to us and pours His grace into our lives. His Spirit does a cleansing, purifying work in our hearts, gives us victory over the noisy, demanding tyrant of self, and enables us to be thankful people, even in the midst of challenging circumstances.

Humble people are wrapped up in Christ. A humble person thinks much of God and others, and little, if at all, of himself. He recognizes that anything he has is better than he deserves. He does not feel anyone owes him anything. He does not feel entitled to have more, or for life to be easy, or for everyone to love him and treat him well. He is grateful for the least little kindness that is extended to him, knowing it is more than he deserves.

Gratitude in Action:

1. Make a list of anything you can recall "whining" about recently. Include things like frustrating people, annoying circumstances, wanting something you couldn't get (e.g., an uninterrupted nap), or having something you wished you didn't have (e.g., a cold). How does your complaining manifest a spirit of pride, entitlement, and expectations?

2. Sit quietly before the Lord for a time today, and say, "I sit on the ground before You." You may even want to literally bow your head down to the ground as you come into His presence, as an expression of your desire to humble yourself before Him. Confess any pride that has shown itself in complaining, irritability, anger, or resentment, rather than giving of thanks. Humbly tell Him that you don't deserve any of His favor, and give Him thanks for any specific recent blessings He brings to mind— including those situations you have complained about! (If a circumstance involves something sinful or evil, ask how He might want to use it in your life to make you more like Jesus.)

Key Thought:

_____

_____

Gratitude List:

_____

_____

Insights:

_____

_____

Scripture Reading: 2 Corinthians 9:6–15

Where gratitude grows, you will generally find generosity flourishing as well. Yet, generosity is a most unnatural quality if ever there was one. I mean, here we stand today, in an age as risky, volatile, and dangerous as any other in memory, where conventional wisdom declares this is no time to be loose with our money and other resources. The financial commentators tell us what our hearts were already thinking: Protect what you can, because tomorrow could all be chaos.

Yet Paul expressed a surprising lack of concern for economic indicators when he advised the Corinthian church to let generosity be among the most notable expressions of their gratitude. His trust in God's supply was so strong, he treated as a "given" the fact that the church would "be enriched in every way for all your generosity, which through us will produce thanksgiving to God" (v. 11). "God is able to make all grace abound to you, so that having all sufficiency in all things at all times, you may abound in every good work" (v. 8). In all things. At all times. Even these times.

Grateful people are generous people. Those who have "freely received," are motivated to "freely give" (Matt. 10:8 NKJV).

Gratitude in Action:

1. Why do gratitude and generosity go hand in hand? Can we truly be defined by one without practicing the other?

2. What act(s) of generosity might gratitude be motivating you toward today? Ask God for wisdom and faith; then follow through on the promptings of His Spirit in relation to your giving.

Key Thought:

_____
_____
_____
_____
_____

Gratitude List:

_____
_____
_____
_____
_____

Insights:

_____
_____
_____
_____
_____

Scripture Reading: 1 Corinthians 2:6–11

Scottish minister Alexander Whyte was known for his uplifting prayers in the pulpit. He always found something for which to be grateful. But one Sunday morning, the weather was so dank and gloomy that the church members said among themselves, "Certainly the preacher won't think of anything to thank the Lord for on such a wretched day." Much to their surprise, however, Whyte stepped to the pulpit that dreary morning and began by praying, "We thank Thee, Lord, that it is not always like this."[1]

There are blessings in your life and mine that "no eye has seen, nor ear heard"— blessings that only show themselves by not showing up. Today, try listing as many of these things to be grateful for as you can think of.

For example, think of the miles you've driven without getting a flat tire. Think of the big tree out front that's never dropped a damaging limb on your house. Think of a destructive sin or habit the Lord has kept you from being tempted by. Perhaps you're hobbled by a medical problem or two, but think of a dozen you've never experienced.

Look at all the benefits on your growing list of gratitude-inducers, and by backing them into reverse like this, you'll find your blessings multiplying at an amazing rate.

Gratitude in Action:

Gratitude can (and should) lead us to intercession. A good prayer starter is to ask God to remind you of those who do suffer from some of the things He's spared you from. Lift these people up to Him today.

Key Thought:

_____

_____

_____

_____

_____

Gratitude List:

_____

_____

_____

_____

_____

Insights:

_____

_____

_____

_____

_____

[1] Paul Lee Tan, _Encyclopedia of 7,700 Illustrations_ (Rockville, MD: Assurance Publishers, 1979), 1456.

Scripture Reading: *Romans 5:1–11*

If you're a Christian, the best thing that's ever happened to you is being saved from sure destruction for your sins and ushered into the family of God, beginning now and continuing for all eternity. Sit and ponder that reality for a while.

Sadly, time tends to dull our appreciation of the magnificent, sacrificial work of Christ on our behalf. Life gets so busy and complicated, we can go for weeks—or longer—without being swept away by the enormity of our salvation.

One of my friends paraphrases the well-known memory verse of Romans 5:8 this way: "God demonstrated His love toward us in this: while we were in open, hostile rebellion toward Him, having no interest in Him—not only that but actively despising Him and all that He stands for—Christ died for us." How can we not be inexpressibly thankful? But praise God, gratitude can reopen the wonder to us, throwing back the dingy curtains of complacency until the full light of His grace and glory come streaming through.

Gratitude in Action:

The salvation we have in Christ is a "many-splendored thing," a diamond with countless brilliant facets. What spiritual blessings in today's Scripture reading need to be added to your list of "Gifts from God"?

Key Thought:

_____

_____

_____

_____

_____

Gratitude List:

_____

_____

_____

_____

_____

Insights:

_____

_____

_____

_____

_____

Day 12: *Gratitude You Can Feel*

Scripture Reading: *3 John 1–4*

Numerous secular studies and research projects testify to the healthy benefits of the attitude of gratitude. The Research Project on Gratitude and Thanksgiving, conducted by two psychologists, broke several hundred people into three groups and required each person to keep a diary. The first group simply recorded events that occurred through the day. The second group was asked to journal negative experiences. The final group made a list each day of things for which they were grateful. The gratitude group reported greater levels of alertness and energy, exercised more frequently, and experienced less depression and stress.[1] From better sleep to fewer medical symptoms, gratitude just seems to satisfy.

The apostle John says to his beloved sons and brothers in Christ, "I pray that all may go well with you and that you may be in good health, as it goes well with your soul." He's right—there's something physically strengthening and sustaining about being joyful in the Lord and grateful for His blessings. While living a godly life does not guarantee physical health, a healthy (spiritual) heart can do much to enhance our physical and emotional well-being. What are some reasons you think that might be the case?

Gratitude in Action:

We've been on this gratitude journey for more than ten days now. What differences have you noticed in your overall wellness and outlook? Add these "benefits" to your journal.

Key Thought:

_____

_____

_____

_____

_____

Gratitude List:

_____

_____

_____

_____

_____

Insights:

_____

_____

_____

_____

_____

[1] R. A. Emmons and M. E. McCullough, "Counting Blessings Versus Burdens: Experimental Studies of Gratitude and Subjective Well-Being in Daily Life," _Journal of Personality and Social Psychology 84_ (2003): 377–389.

Scripture Reading: *Psalm 43:1–5*

The Psalms are a good place to camp out if your heart's desire is to be grateful—though not because they're filled with nothing but happy, upbeat sentiments. It surprises many who embark on a journey of the Psalms to find that they vibrate with every emotion known to man. They speak of back-breaking pressures, deep valleys of depression, times when life barely seems worth living. And yet, as we see in today's reading, the Psalms reveal that the only ultimate answer to trouble, grief, pain, and loss is a constant returning to God in worship and gratitude. Every other semi-solution proves empty and short-lived, incapable of infusing real hope into life's unbearable situations.

"Why are you cast down, O my soul, and why are you in turmoil within me? Hope in God; for I shall again praise him, my salvation and my God" (Ps. 43:5). "My flesh and my heart may fail, but God is the strength of my heart and my portion forever" (73:26). "For his anger is but for a moment, and his favor is for a lifetime. Weeping may tarry for the night, but joy comes in the morning" (30:5).

Your heart may be crying out, "Oh God, let it be morning!" Keep hoping in Him until the day finally dawns. Even in the darkest night, you can still experience His peace and rest, knowing that the joy of morning is ahead. Resolve not to let your joy level be determined by the presence or absence of storms, but by the presence of God. Choose to be joyful in Him today.

Gratitude in Action:

Choose a few Psalms—even if only at random—to read throughout the day today (aloud if possible). See if they don't cause praise and thanks to well up in your heart.

Key Thought:

_____

_____

_____

_____

_____

Gratitude List:

_____

_____

_____

_____

_____

Insights:

_____

_____

_____

_____

_____

Scripture Reading: *Psalm 56*

Psalm 56 is a hymn of praise and trust, of confidence and strength, of worship and gratitude. If your Bible includes inscriptions at the beginning of selected Psalms, though, you'll notice that this particular one was written in far less than ideal circumstances.

David was on the run from King Saul, and when spotted and seized by the Philistines in the city of Gath, he had faked insanity to avoid being detained. This was definitely a desperate man in desperate straits.

Yet in the midst of intense, frightening hardship, he submitted himself to the Lord's protection, and found within this relationship the ability to say, "When I am afraid, I trust in you. . . . What can flesh do to me?" (vv. 3–4). He didn't deny the reality of what was happening to him, but he found reason to be grateful even for his sorrows, knowing that the Lord was catching every one of his tears in a bottle (v. 8).

The bottom line for David in this experience: "I will render thank offerings to you. For you have delivered my soul from death, yes, my feet from falling, that I may walk before God in the light of life" (vv. 12–13).

Perhaps it's hard for you to find much to be thankful for today. Perhaps all you can see is what's wrong, what hurts, and what others are doing to you. But look above your circumstances, beyond your fears, and ask God to show you what He's doing in the midst of them.

Gratitude in Action:

Look back through your list of blessings and benefits, adding any new ones that come to mind. Focus on the ones that give you the most comfort in crisis.

Key Thought:

_____

_____

_____

_____

_____

Gratitude List:

_____

_____

_____

_____

_____

Insights:

_____

_____

_____

_____

_____

Scripture Reading: Psalm 50:14–15, 23

As you know, giving thanks sometimes requires a sacrifice. Plenty of occasions exist in life where being thankful is the last thing you feel like doing, where nothing seems good or gratitude-worthy.

The last few days' readings have been leading up to this, and though this is a hard task to undertake, I pray that you will open your heart to the Lord and choose to embrace it. Today, I'd like you to make a list of all the difficult things in your life right now. Spell them out, as detailed as you'd like to express them.

Then, when you get through writing, I want you to classify these not as burdens and impossibilities. Rather, I urge you to use this list as a prompt for giving thanks.

That assignment may seem strange—or impossible! We are not expected to thank God *"for"* things that are sinful. But we can give thanks *"in* everything," knowing that God is still God and He uses all things in this fallen world to accomplish His purposes, one of which is the sanctification of His children.

Yes, to give thanks as you consider the list before you will be a sacrifice. You probably won't *feel* like making this sacrifice. But it will be pleasing to the Lord. And what's more, His promise to those who make gratitude their practice is that He will "show [them] the salvation of God" (v. 23). When gratitude becomes your newly adopted attitude and lifestyle—even in the midst of pressures and problems—you will see His deliverance in new and amazing ways.

Begin to track the ways that God is using these circumstances in your life. Perhaps they are causing you to become more dependent on Him, or to call upon Him in prayer, or to exercise faith in His promises.

When we call upon our Lord "in the day of trouble" (v. 15), with minds set on glorifying Him, He does marvelous things in the midst of our pain and sorrow. Thank Him by faith that He can use each of these situations as a means to display His glory.

Gratitude in Action:

Pray over any painful situations and broken relationships on your list. Ask God for tailor-made grace and for wisdom regarding each one. Then, rather than complaining about them, ask Him to show you how to turn them into praises. Open your heart to receive them as opportunities for His grace to shine through.

Key Thought:

_____

_____

_____

_____

Gratitude List:

_____

_____

_____

_____

Insights:

_____

_____

_____

_____

Day 16: *Sing and Give Thanks*

Scripture Reading: Psalm 30

My mother was an extraordinarily gifted, classically-trained singer. I, on the other hand, apparently inherited my dad's genes in that area. By most anyone's standards, he had a poor singing voice. But he used the voice he had to sing praises aloud. He was not timid or self-conscious when he sang and gave no indication of being concerned about what others thought! I am grateful for his example and have tried to emulate it.

Unlike most other religions, Christianity is a "singing" faith. The word "sing" occurs over one hundred times in the Bible—more than sixty of them in the book of Psalms alone. Psalms has appropriately been called the "hymn book of ancient Israel." The psalmists sometimes sang songs of lament and longing. But most often they sang songs of praise and thanks to God. Verses 4 and 12 in today's Scripture reading both tie singing and giving thanks together.

I've often pondered why the Scripture places such emphasis on praising the Lord with singing, and why it is that all believers are commanded to sing to the Lord, regardless of their natural ability—or lack thereof. There are a number of illustrations in the Scripture of the powerful effect of praise through music. (For starters, try 2 Chronicles 20:21–23, where God gave a great victory to the Israelites after the choir held a praise service at the front of the troops marching into battle!)

There is no doubt that the devil despises God-ward praise. We have some reason to believe that at one time, before pride caused him to lose his position, he may have been one of the "worship leaders" in heaven and therefore is particularly repulsed and repelled when God's people praise Him with singing and musical instruments.

When I talk with a woman who is struggling with chronic discouragement or depression, I often ask two questions: (1) Are you memorizing Scripture? and (2) Are you singing to the Lord? I'm not suggesting these are magic "pills" that will make every emotional struggle go away, but I have found these two means of grace to be extremely effective at recalibrating my heart and restoring inner peace.

I have often experienced fresh springs of God's grace as I have exercised faith in singing to Him in praise and thanksgiving. At times, when I am deeply distraught or discouraged, I will open my hymnal and just begin to sing. Songs like "Leaning on the Everlasting Arms" or "Tis So Sweet to Trust in Jesus" (all stanzas!). Occasionally I am crying so hard I can scarcely get the words out. But as I sing to the Lord, my heart and mind are re-tethered to His goodness and love, and invariably, the cloud begins to lift. In fact, I sing *until* the cloud lifts.

Gratitude in Action:

1. As today's reading exhorts us, *"Sing praises to the LORD . . . and give thanks to his holy name"* (v. 4)! Whether it's a cloudy or sunny day in your heart, sing! Right now, if possible. Put on a CD or listen to your iPod and sing along with others, or just sing to Him on your own—the Lord will love your "joyful sound"!

2. Sing praise choruses that are familiar to you, or pull out a hymnal and sing some of those rich hymns by Charles Wesley, Isaac Watts, Fanny Crosby, or Frances Havergal that we don't sing often enough anymore.

Key Thought:

_____

_____

Gratitude List:

_____

_____

Insights:

_____

_____

Scripture Reading: Proverbs 3:13–18

We've spent a few days in the Psalms, letting gratitude continue to grow in us as we see God's people of old choose thanksgiving over bitterness.

Choosing to be grateful is a decision rooted in godly wisdom, a theme highlighted in the book of Proverbs. I've heard wisdom described as "skill in everyday living." And training our hearts to be grateful for the blessings of God that we experience is linked to our pursuit of godly wisdom in every area of our lives.

When the writer of Proverbs outlines the benefits of wisdom, he is also advertising the benefits of every other habit and discipline inspired by the Scriptures. And since the practice of being thankful is a basic characteristic of God's people, I believe these passages that call us to wise, godly living can appropriately be applied to the issue of gratitude as well.

That's why I really like what's implied in today's reading. It begins and ends with a word—"blessed"—that portrays the type of person God desires and enables us to be. Some translations of the Bible use a slightly different word that helps us better understand what God is offering us, what He promises to those who choose wisdom and gratitude, who choose to accept and believe that His ways are to be desired above all others. That word is "happy."

For most people, *happiness* is tied to circumstances—to what is *happening* in their lives. For Christians, however, happiness or blessedness is not dependent on the weather, the stock market, or how our last haircut turned out. Real happiness—that unshakable sense of peace, contentment, and well-being—comes as we remind ourselves of the blessings we have in Christ, and then respond with thankfulness.

I want that kind of happiness, don't you? And apparently God wants it for us, too. He wants us to experience the deep, inner happiness that is the lot of those who are completely satisfied with Christ.

So as we're seeking the Lord for grateful hearts, let's not be surprised to see ourselves smiling a little more than usual, being more easily contented, and happy with God and what He is accomplishing in us.

Gratitude in Action:

We've talked about being "loud" with our thanksgiving, being vocal about what God is doing. Check to be sure your countenance is also expressing a joyful, thankful heart.

Key Thought:

_____

_____

_____

_____

Gratitude List:

_____

_____

_____

_____

Insights:

_____

_____

_____

_____

Scripture Reading: 1 Corinthians 10:1–13

In today's reading, Paul reflects back on the children of Israel in the wilderness and identifies four specific sins they committed, all of which had dire consequences. What are those four sins?

- v. 7
- v. 8
- v. 9
- v. 10

All of these sins resulted in tragic outcomes. We can understand God punishing idolatry and sexual immorality. But it's sobering to realize that He includes the sin of "grumbling" (your translation may say "murmur" or "complain") with these other sins and takes them all seriously!

The sin referred to in 1 Corinthians 10:10 relates to incidents recorded in Numbers 11:1; 14:1–28; 16:11–35. Take a few moments to skim through these passages to give you some context.

Every time I read these Old Testament accounts, I am convicted of how my murmuring and complaining displeases the Lord (and how merciful He is not to judge me as He did the Israelites!).

Grumbling is the opposite of thankfulness. Like gratitude, it starts in the heart and expresses itself in our words. It grows out of the sin of discontentment—not being satisfied with what God has provided.

Philippians 2:14–15 says we are to "do *all* things without grumbling," and that when we are obedient in this matter, our lives shine the light of Christ into our dark world.

Are you guilty of the sin of grumbling? If so, confess that to the Lord; ask Him to forgive you and to grant you true repentance. Purpose in your heart to "put off" all complaining and to "put on" a heart of thankfulness.

Gratitude in Action:

Ask God to make you sensitive and alert to situations over the next twenty-four hours where your natural response would be to murmur or whine. Ask Him for grace to *give thanks* every time you're tempted to grumble. (If you have a pattern of complaining, it probably won't disappear in a day! This is one exercise you'll need to do intentionally day after day, until your "default response" has changed from grumbling to gratitude.)

Key Thought:

_____

_____

_____

_____

Gratitude List:

_____

_____

_____

_____

Insights:

_____

_____

_____

_____

Scripture Reading: Romans 8:1; 1 Corinthians 1:4; Ephesians 1:15–16; Philippians 1:3–4; Colossians 1:3–4; 1 Thessalonians 1:2–3; 2 Thessalonians 1:3

The apostle Paul was a grateful man. That's because he never forgot where God found him. He never forgot how greatly he had sinned against the holiness and the law of God and the church of Jesus Christ. And he never got over the wonder of the amazing grace of God that had reached down to him, undeserving as he was. His life is a great illustration of the principle that "guilt + grace → gratitude."

When you read Paul's New Testament letters to various believers and churches, you can't help but notice his many expressions of gratitude for spiritual blessings lavished on those who are in Christ: the grace of God, the saving work of Christ, forgiveness of sin, the gift of the Spirit, the privilege of ministry—the list is lengthy.

If you took time to read the verses listed above, you also couldn't help but notice that Paul was thankful for *others*—especially for brothers and sisters in Christ, fellow servants, ministry partners. In his correspondence (and he was quite the letter writer!), Paul didn't just leave it at generalized expressions of gratitude—he often took time to identify specific individuals for whom he was grateful and to let them know how much he appreciated their contribution to his life and ministry.

The most extensive such list is found in Romans 16:1–16. In fact, why not turn there now and read through that passage (you probably haven't meditated on this one for awhile!). As you read, underline in your Bible or make a list in your journal of words or phrases that describe what Paul was grateful for in these believers in Rome.

Most of the names in this list—many of them hard to pronounce—represent people about whom we know little or nothing. From a human perspective, none of them attained to the "position" or "importance" Paul had as an apostle. Why did Paul think it necessary, inspired by the Holy Spirit, to take valuable time and space to write this lengthy passage? I think one reason is that he saw these people as provisions of God's grace. And he knew no one is self-sufficient—we need each other and our lives are enriched and blessed by other like-hearted believers.

People matter to God. And they should matter to us. It's important to take time to recognize and express appreciation for the contributions that even little-known people make to His kingdom and to our lives.

Inspired by the example of the apostle Paul and others, I've tried to make it a point over the years to stop and take stock periodically of my "gratitude accounts"—to make sure they're "caught up" and to find meaningful ways to express gratitude for and to the people who have contributed to my life. I'm sure those expressions encourage the recipients. But they also provide a much-needed antidote in my own life to pride, independence, isolation, and self-reliance.

Gratitude in Action:

1. Make a list in your journal of individuals who have blessed or touched your life in some way. To help you get started . . . how about: the person who introduced you to Jesus, your parents, other family members, pastors, teachers, coaches, friends, coworkers, neighbors, authors, leaders of Christian ministries—you get the idea.

   As you write each name, ask yourself, *Have I ever thanked this person for the way God has used him/her in my life?* Put a checkmark next to each individual to whom you have expressed gratitude.

2. Begin the process of catching up on your "gratitude accounts." Don't try to tackle the whole list at once. Pick one for starters. In the next twenty-four hours, write a letter, make a call, compose an email—find a way to express your gratitude for that person's influence and impact in your life.* Then move to the next one . . . and the next . . . until you've expressed gratitude to each person on your list. By that time, there will undoubtedly be new people to add to the list! And—you can always start over again with the same list.

Key Thought:

_____

_____

_____

* Check out www.reviveourhearts.com/choosinggratitude to find some attractive note cards designed for this purpose

Scripture Reading: 1 Timothy 5:8; 2 Timothy 1:3–5; 3:14–15

It seems that it's often easier to express gratitude for and to people we hardly know than for and to those in our own family. Maybe that's because we know our family members so well (and they know us!). Or it may be that we really do appreciate them, but we've come to take them for granted.

Godly character in every area of our lives will show up within the four walls of our homes. We can't say we love God, if we don't manifest His love to our family members or if we allow bitterness to fester in our hearts toward them.

For the most part, we don't get to choose our family members, as we do our "friends." Yet we are called to love and care for those in our families, in spite of their personalities, their idiosyncrasies, or their character flaws. And that's not always easy!

Timothy had a godly mother and grandmother (not hard to be thankful for them). We don't know much about Timothy's father, but many Bible scholars believe that he was probably not a believer. He may or may not have been supportive of the faith of his wife and son. But it was no accident that Timothy grew up in the family he did. Though it was probably not an "ideal" home situation (what home situation is ideal?!), he still had much in his family for which to be grateful.

Regardless of your family heritage, it's important to realize that your relatives are not the result of "genetic chance," but that you have been placed into the family of God's sovereign choosing for you, and that He wants to use your family—rough edges and all—as a means to sanctify you and conform you into the likeness of His Son. Embracing that truth will help you cultivate a grateful heart for those who make up your family.

Gratitude in Action:

1. Today, focus on expressing gratitude for and to your family members. In your journal, make a list of each member of your immediate family (mate, parents, children, siblings, etc.). Then next to each name write one quality

about their life for which you are particularly grateful.

2. Take time to thank God for each member of the family He has given you. Then pick one or two individuals from your list to whom you can express gratitude today, in person, by phone, or with a note or email. You might want to start by saying something like this:

> *Today, I thanked God for you. And I wanted to tell you how grateful I am that you are part of my family, and especially for this particular quality I see in your life . . .*

(Note: You may want to express gratitude to a family member who has been especially difficult to love!)

Key Thought:

_____

_____

_____

_____

Gratitude List:

_____

_____

_____

Insights:

_____

_____

_____

_____

Day 21: *Family Matters*

Scripture Reading: *Proverbs 21:2–9*

If you were faithful to read the above passage, you can probably guess which verse I wanted to highlight: "It is better to live in a corner of the housetop than in a house shared with a quarrelsome wife" (v. 9). And, yes, I am serious about the dangers posed by tongues that are contentious, combative, and discontented.

But while heeding this as a warning, let's also turn it into a positive. If one of the blessings of gratitude is that it makes us generally happier people, it follows that gratitude makes those who live with us happier, too.

Let the first halves of these proverbs become as desirable to you as the second halves are detestable: "The wisest of women builds her house, but folly with her own hands tears it down" (Prov. 14:1). "A gentle tongue is a tree of life, but perverseness in it breaks the spirit" (15:4). "An excellent wife is the crown of her husband, but she who brings shame is like rottenness in his bones" (12:4).

The restorative power of a grateful heart and tongue is more potent than we can imagine, as is the destructive potential of being bitter and difficult to live with. "Gracious words are like a honeycomb, sweetness to the soul and health to the body" (Prov. 16:24). Let's make sure our words have that kind of effect.

Gratitude in Action:

Ask God to guard your heart—and your tongue—today. Any time you hear yourself saying words that are contentious, complaining, or critical, rather than gracious, gentle, and godly . . . stop. Ask Him to forgive you. And seek forgiveness from those to whom—or in whose presence—you spoke.

Key Thought:

_____

_____

_____

_____

_____

Gratitude List:

_____

_____

_____

_____

_____

Insights:

_____

_____

_____

_____

_____

Scripture Reading: Proverbs 30:7–9

Gratitude and contentment are not the same thing, but they are close enough cousins that it's helpful to see them working together in our hearts. This passage from the Proverbs is one that unites them in a most compelling way.

You may have heard some preachers and teachers leave the impression that God intends for every Christian to be materially rich. Others, though, swing the pendulum too far the other way, proudly wearing poverty like a cloak of self-righteous sainthood. Today's proverb puts a proper perspective on the whole thing.

The Word is teaching us to focus less on our climb up or down the economic ladder and more on being grateful for where we are—not only because to do otherwise would be sinful and proud, but also because we don't know what the Lord may be saving us from by not giving us everything we might want. Even if we possess much less than others have, if our hearts are full of gratitude, neither money nor the lack of it can shake our contented dependence on God.

Gratitude in Action:

Money isn't everything, but our desire for it and the things it buys can certainly squash the vibrancy of our gratitude. Ask the Lord to show you if there is any root of discontentment or "love of money" in your heart. Ask Him to provide just what He knows you need—enough to keep you from being tempted to sin to get your needs met, but not so much that you no longer need to rely on Him as your Provider. Take some time to thank Him for His practical, material provision in your life today.

Key Thought:

_____

_____

_____

_____

_____

Gratitude List:

_____

_____

_____

_____

_____

Insights:

_____

_____

_____

_____

_____

Scripture Reading: 1 Timothy 6:6–10

Andrew Carnegie, the wealthy industrialist whose fortune rivaled that of any other contemporary at the time of his death in 1919, left a million dollars to one of his relatives, who in return became angry and bitter toward his generous benefactor because Mr. Carnegie had also left $365 million dollars to charitable causes.

On its face, we can hardly believe this. How can a person have a million reasons to be grateful yet find it hundreds of millions short of being adequate? But don't we all possess some sense of entitlement toward God? How often does our expectation or demand for "more" tower over the plenty we already possess?

That's because we forget that God doesn't owe us anything. We are debtors. We are the ones who owe. We think we deserve more (or different or better) than we have, and therefore we forget or minimize the blessings God has already given and continues to give. Not content with food, clothing, and a roof over our heads, we whine if we don't have a certain kind of house, a certain kind of car, a certain kind of job, a certain kind of marriage, and certain kinds of friends living in a certain kind of neighborhood and income bracket.

The fact is, we're often not so different than Carnegie's ungrateful beneficiary. It's time we let gratitude be our ticket to freedom. It's true—being grateful can lead us to a place of simple satisfaction.

Gratitude in Action:

What kinds of "wants" are you defining as "needs"? Ask God to show you any ways you may have become blinded to His grace. Highlight them. Confess them. And trade them in on the bounty God promises to the grateful.

Key Thought:

_____
_____
_____
_____
_____

Gratitude List:

_____
_____
_____
_____
_____

Insights:

_____
_____
_____
_____
_____

Day 24: *A Woman after God's Heart*

Scripture Reading: *Ruth 2:1–13*

Speaking of good examples to follow, the biblical account of Ruth is one that I find particularly moving and instructive every time I read it. Ruth was a woman with a humble heart—a trait we've identified as a companion virtue of gratitude. She didn't claim her rights. She didn't insist that Boaz provide her a living by letting her glean in his fields. And because she relinquished her demands for certain expectations, she was able to be genuinely thankful when she actually did receive the blessing of his generosity. Verses 10 and 13 are not a show of false flattery but the expressions of a heart operating out of humble gratitude.

Too many of us live with a chip on our shoulder, as if the world owes us something. "You ought to do this for me. You ought to serve me. You ought to meet my needs." But the humble heart—the grateful heart—says, "I don't deserve this, and it's an amazing act of grace that you should minister to my needs."

I once journaled the following prayer after meditating on Ruth's story: "O God, please take me back to see where you found me and where I would be today apart from You. Please strip me of my proud, demanding ways and clothe me in meekness, humility, and gratitude. Empty me of myself and fill me with the sweet, gracious nature of Jesus Christ."

Ruth just went out to serve with a humble, thankful heart. And as a result, God made sure her needs were met. He'll do the same for you.

Gratitude in Action:

1. Who do you know who consistently exhibits a grateful spirit? What is it about them that makes them so remarkable? What can you learn from their example?

2. Journal your own prayer in response to Ruth's example. Ask God to help you exemplify Ruth's kind of character.

Key Thought:

_____

_____

_____

_____

_____

Gratitude List:

_____

_____

_____

_____

Insights:

_____

_____

_____

_____

_____

Scripture Reading: *Deuteronomy 8:1–10*

Historians have differing perspectives in relation to the first Thanksgiving celebrations in America. But there are some details we know for sure to be true. We know that the Pilgrims' journey from Holland to England to the New World was frightfully difficult, with sickness and storms their frequent visitors on the arduous, weeks-long voyage. We know that once they arrived, the task of carving dwellings out of the forest quick enough to hold back the advancing effects of winter was a losing race against time. Nearly half of those who made the trip didn't survive the stay. The Pilgrims certainly built more graves than huts.

And yet with sheer survival the order of each day, and with fears for their families an all-consuming worry, their writings and recorded history are filled with demonstrations and attitudes of thanksgiving.

Each Sunday—from the first landing of the *Mayflower* through the repeating years of their little colony, in lean times as well as relatively plentiful—they gathered for prayer, meditation, the singing of hymns, and a sermon. It was their regular practice to stop and give thanks to God at the outset of each week.

Though having to be restricted to half-rations when their stores of crops proved insufficient for the first, long winters, William Bradford commented that they were learning by experience "the truth of the word in Deuteronomy 8:3—that man lives not by bread alone, but by every word that proceeds out of the mouth of the Lord."[1]

And when the years began slowly bringing a renewed abundance of harvests, rather than telling God they could manage just fine by themselves from here on, Edward Winslow wrote, "Having these many signs of God's favor and [acceptance], we thought it would be a great ingratitude if secretly we should content ourselves with private thanksgiving. . . . Therefore, another solemn day [referring back to a day of prayer and fasting they had observed earlier in the summer] was set apart and appointed for that end; wherein we returned glory, honor, and praise, with all thankfulness to our God who dealt so graciously with us. . . ."[2]

What a wonderful example those early Pilgrims provide of choosing gratitude in times of plenty and times of want!

Gratitude in Action:

Use your prayer time today to think back over the history of God's faithfulness in your life, your family, and your church. Make a list of desperate situations or seasons when you have witnessed His providential protection and provision.

Key Thought:

_____

_____

_____

_____

Gratitude List:

_____

_____

_____

_____

Insights:

_____

_____

[1] Nathaniel Philbrick and Thomas Philbrick , eds., *The Mayflower Papers: Selected Writings of Colonial New England* (New York: Penguin Classics, 2007), 34.

[2] Edward Winslow, *Good Newes from New England,* [1624], ed. Alexander Young (Bedford, MA: Applewood Books, 1996), 54–56.

Scripture Reading: *Ezra 3:8–13*

On October 3, 1863, at the height of the Civil War, President Abraham Lincoln issued a Proclamation of Thanksgiving, calling the nation to observe a "day of Thanksgiving and Praise." This proclamation eventually led to the establishing of our national day of Thanksgiving.

The document began by listing multiple blessings the nation had experienced through the course of the year, even in the midst of a severe conflict. It called the American people to recognize the Source of those blessings and to respond collectively to the Giver in gratitude, repentance, and intercession. Here's an excerpt:

> No human counsel hath devised nor hath any mortal hand worked out these great things. They are the gracious gifts of the Most High God, who, while dealing with us in anger for our sins, hath nevertheless remembered mercy.
>
> It has seemed to me fit and proper that they should be solemnly, reverently and gratefully acknowledged as with one heart and one voice by the whole American People. I do therefore invite my fellow citizens in every part of the United States . . . to set apart and observe the last Thursday of November next, as a day of Thanksgiving and Praise to our beneficent Father who dwelleth in the Heavens.
>
> And I recommend to them that . . . they do also, with humble penitence for our national perverseness and disobedience . . . fervently implore the interposition of the Almighty Hand to heal the wounds of the nation and to restore it as soon as may be consistent with the Divine purposes to the full enjoyment of peace, harmony, tranquillity and Union.

Set against a background of divisive conflict, our nation's leader in the 1860s was humble enough to know that our nation needed God . . . and needed to be grateful. This kind of heart is no less needed in our nation today than it was then.

The call to gratitude goes beyond the church and into every avenue of life. Pray today for a humble, grateful, repentant spirit to be birthed in our own hearts, and among our leaders at every level.

Gratitude in Action:

1. You may not consider yourself to be much of a writer. That's okay. But today I want you to try crafting your own declaration of thanksgiving. Use some of the insights the Lord has been growing in you these last few weeks. Incorporate some of the Scriptures that have particularly touched you. And dedicate your life to what these words of yours are saying. Make this your own declaration of thanksgiving in your heart and home.

2. It's not enough to keep this to yourself. Share what you've written with your family or a close friend. Post it on Facebook, send an email to your friends. Be an igniter of gratitude by encouraging those you love and care about to cultivate a thankful heart.

Key Thought:

_____

_____

_____

Gratitude List:

_____

_____

_____

Insights:

_____

_____

_____

Scripture Reading: 1 Timothy 4:11–16

We're nearing the end of our month-long journey into gratitude. To help you measure what kind of effect this experience is having on your life, take a little quiz today to see where you're growing and where you still need work. Try answering these questions candidly in your journal—not just yes or no, but with supporting details that come to mind:

1. Do I often complain about my circumstances, feeling like I deserve better?

2. Do others hear me voice more complaints and negative comments than words of gratitude about the typical events of daily life?

3. Would others describe me as a thankful person?

4. What evidence is there that I have a grateful or an ungrateful spirit?

5. How often do I begin statements with these words: "I am so thankful that. . ."?

6. Do I more frequently display a pessimistic, negative outlook or a positive, grateful perspective?

7. Am I reserved or eager when it comes to expressing appreciation to others?

8. My most recent expression of gratitude was . . .

Gratitude in Action:

Through the course of writing this devotional, God has done a fresh work in my own heart in the area of gratitude. But I had to be willing to humble myself, confess my need, and ask for prayer, help, and accountability from those close to me. Remember, our hearts cannot change apart from His grace giving us the desire and the power to please Him. And God pours out His grace on the humble.

If you haven't done so already, consider taking this gratitude challenge into an accountability setting, letting others help you stay true to your commitment, while being there to offer your support to them, as well.

Key Thought:

_____

_____

_____

_____

Gratitude List:

_____

_____

_____

_____

Insights:

_____

_____

_____

_____

Scripture Reading: *Philippians 1:3–11*

I have found that anything I fail to plan into my day usually doesn't get done. If I don't start the morning realizing that some particular thing is a priority, my mind isn't likely to remember it once the everyday pressures start squeezing everything else out of their way.

If expressing gratitude is to become a way of life for us, we can't treat it as an optional exercise. If it never gets beyond our wish list, if it nestles down with all the other nice things we hope to get around to someday, the "someday" of gratitude will never roll around on our calendars. It will remain a sweet intention, but not a consistent practice.

So I want to encourage you to think of gratitude as being a debt you owe, the same way you're called upon to pay your monthly bills. I'd like to see you open a section in your journal that's designated for "Gratitude Accounts," specific listings of individuals to whom you owe a debt of thanks.

By doing this, you can make it a point today to make a phone call just to thank a friend for the way she's shown her concern for you during a difficult time. You'll be reminded that when you see a certain person at the gym this afternoon, you need to be sure to thank her for helping you stay true to your fitness goals. When the Lord opens a window of opportunity for you to jot a quick thank-you note this evening, you'll have a ready-made list of people to choose from.

We all have gratitude accounts. There just aren't many of us who keep them paid up. Make sure you're becoming the type of person who stays current on your bill.

Gratitude in Action:

1. Who needs to be added to your gratitude account? What gratitude debt do you need to pay *today*?

Key Thought:

_____

_____

_____

_____

_____

Gratitude List:

_____

_____

_____

_____

Insights:

_____

_____

_____

_____

_____

Day 29: *Growing Grateful Children*

Scripture Reading: *Deuteronomy 6:1–12*

Like anything that God is growing in us, His intention in helping us become more like Christ is not merely to benefit ourselves but to help us inspire the same in others, to show them the blessings inherent in trusting the Lord.

If you have been favored with children, you know that gratitude—like most every other character trait—doesn't come naturally for them. But few things are more remarkable (and unusual) in children today than when they're known for their thankful, contented spirit. It is a quality worth every ounce of effort we make to instill it in them.

And while teaching and instruction have their place in growing gratitude in our kids, the best teacher of all (of course) is our example. Do your children hear you thank your husband when he tackles a home repair or gets the car lubed? Do they hear you express gratitude to the Lord and to others for both little and big things throughout the day? Do you tell them how grateful you are for their dad, for your church and your pastor, for their teachers, for the house the Lord has provided for your family, for good health, and for God's abundant blessings to your family? Conversely, do they hear you grumble when your husband delays dinner by needing to see one extra client or when you get a flat tire or the sun doesn't come out for a week?

Gratitude joins many other important virtues that are more effectively caught than taught. How contagious are you, especially at home?

Gratitude in Action:

1. Sit down and talk with your children about the high value God places on gratitude. Tell them how they're going to start seeing some "gratitudinal" changes in you.

2. You may not have children of your own. Who has God placed in your sphere of influence? What are you teaching them about gratitude by your lifestyle?

Key Thought:

_____
_____
_____
_____
_____

Gratitude List:

_____
_____
_____
_____
_____

Insights:

_____
_____
_____
_____
_____

Scripture Reading: *Galatians 5:16–24*

As we begin to launch out on a new lifestyle of gratitude, let's use today to set some goals for what we want God to accomplish in our hearts, being specific about the ways we intend to practice ongoing thankfulness.

For example, if you want to become more deliberate about writing thank-you notes, how many would you like to send in a typical week or month? What Scriptures do you plan to memorize and meditate on in relation to thankfulness? Who will you ask to hold you accountable for specific areas where you need to grow in the grace of gratitude?

Remember, these are not added burdens tacked on to further complicate your day and put a drain on your time. As believers, we've been released from the oppressive demands of the law. As those who are in Christ, we are free to pursue godly living as our glad response to grace received. And we are enabled by the power of His Spirit to obey His will from our hearts. Resist every attempt of the enemy to enslave you, even to good habits and activities.

As you grow in gratitude, you will be so blessed by its reward and spiritual significance, you won't feel as though it's an effort to accomplish it. Whatever mechanics it requires to get it up and running will soon fall away to the freedom of pursuing it with passion.

Are you ready to experience the life-changing power of Christian gratitude? Then let the Lord help you decide what your next steps should be.

Gratitude in Action:

1. Be bold and exercise faith, but don't be afraid to take short strides as you make this your manner of living. Do try, though, to be as specific as you can in plotting your gratitude plan.

2. Write a simple prayer, expressing to the Lord your desire to develop a radically grateful lifestyle. Thank Him for His supernatural grace that will enable you to "abound in thanksgiving."

Key Thought:

_____

_____

_____

_____

_____

Gratitude List:

_____

_____

_____

_____

_____

Insights:

_____

_____

_____

_____

_____

Revive Our Hearts™

Through its various outreaches and the teaching ministry of
Nancy DeMoss Wolgemuth, *Revive Our Hearts* is calling women
around the world to freedom, fullness, and fruitfulness in Christ.

Offering sound, biblical teaching and encouragement for women through . . .

Books & Resources Nancy's books, True Woman Books,
and a wide range of audio/video

Broadcasting Two daily, nationally syndicated broadcasts
(*Revive Our Hearts* and *Seeking Him*) reaching some one
million listeners a week

Events & Training True Woman Conferences and events
designed to equip women's ministry leaders and pastors' wives

Internet ReviveOurHearts.com, TrueWoman.com, and
LiesYoungWomenBelieve.com, daily blogs, and a large,
searchable collection of electronic resources for women in
every season of life

**Believing God for a grassroots movement of authentic revival and
biblical womanhood . . . Encouraging women to:**

- Discover and embrace God's design and mission for their lives.
- Reflect the beauty and heart of Jesus Christ to their world.
- Intentionally pass on the baton of truth to the next generation.
- Pray earnestly for an outpouring of God's Spirit in their families,
  churches, nation, and world.

You can visit us at **ReviveOurHearts.com.** We'd love to hear from you!